P9-BYF-550

WITHDRAWN

Fact Finders®

SCARY
SCIENCE

DANGEROUS DISEASES

SCARY ILLNESSES THAT FRIGHTEN THE WORLD

BY KRISTINE CARLSON ASSELIN

CONSULTANT:
MITCHELL WALKOWICZ, PHD
DEPARTMENT OF MICROBIOLOGY
THE UNIVERSITY OF MASSACHUSETTS AMHERST

CAPSTONE PRESS
a capstone imprint

Fact Finders Books are published by Capstone Press,
1710 Roe Crest Drive, North Mankato, Minnesota 56003
www.capstonepub.com

Copyright © 2014 by Capstone Press, a Capstone imprint. All rights reserved. No part of this publication may
be reproduced in whole or in part, or stored in a retrieval system, or transmitted in any form or by any means,
electronic, mechanical, photocopying, recording, or otherwise, without written permission of the publisher.

Library of Congress Cataloging-in-Publication Data
Asselin, Kristine Carlson.
Dangerous diseases : scary illnesses that frighten the world / by Kristine Carlson Asselin.
pages cm.—(Fact finders. Scary science)
Audience: 8-12.
Audience: Grade 4 to 6.
Includes bibliographical references and index.
Summary: "Describes various diseases and epidemics that have occurred around the world"—Provided
by publisher.
ISBN 978-1-4765-3927-0 (library binding) — ISBN 978-1-4765-5125-8 (pbk.) —
 ISBN 978-1-4765-5974-2 (ebook pdf)
1. Communicable diseases—History—Juvenile literature. 2. Emerging infectious diseases—Juvenile literature.
3. Epidemics—History—Juvenile literature. I. Title. II. Title: Dangerous and unexplained diseases.
RA643.A84 2014
362.1969—dc23   2013022095

Editorial Credits
Jennifer Besel, editor; Veronica Scott, designer; Marcie Spence, media researcher;
    Eric Manske, production specialist

Photo Credits
Alamy Images: Everett Collection Inc., 15, Image Asset Management Ltd., 9, Medical-on-Line, 17, Nucleus
Medical Art Inc., 23; AP Images: AP Photo, cover; Corbis: Dr. Ken Greer/Visuals Unlimited, 11, Karen
Kasmauski/Science Faction, 10, 26; Getty Images: Alfred Eisenstaedt/Time & Life Pictures, 19, DEA/A. Dagli
Orti/De Agostini, 6, Matt Cardy, 27, Paul Thompson/FPG, 8, Raphael Gaillarde/Gamma-Rapho, 24; Science
Source: Mike Devlin, 12, Sue Ford, 21; Shutterstock: anyaivanova, 28-29, artcalin, design element, fusebulb, 4,
Heiko Kiera, 22, kentoh, design element, martynowi.cz, 5, mrfiza, 20, Triff, design element, Vectroific, design
element; Visuals Unlimited: Carol & Mike Werner, 25

Printed in the United States of America in Stevens Point, Wisconsin.
092013 007769WZS14

TABLE OF CONTENTS

CHAPTER 1

MAKING YOU SICK

Germs live all around us. They live on food, in water, and on countertops. They even squiggle inside your body. Most of these germs, or microbes, don't bother you at all.

But a few of these creatures are monsters. Some microbes can make your stomach heave or cause pus-filled bumps all over your skin. These monstrous microbes come in two varieties—bacteria and viruses.

Bacteria are single-celled microbes that thrive in all types of environments. Most bacteria won't harm people. In fact some help digest your supper or fight off a cold. But a few kinds can spell trouble for your body.

microbe—a tiny living thing that is too small to be seen without a microscope

gene—a part of every cell that carries physical and behavioral information passed from parents to their children

Unlike bacteria, viruses can't live just anywhere. They need to live inside a human body, plant, or animal to survive. Once inside a body, viruses attach themselves to healthy cells and take over.

Viruses and bacteria cause most illnesses. But they're not the only things that make people sick. Even our **genes** can cause problems. And doctors are still trying to find the causes for other diseases. Are you ready to explore some scary science?

A COMPUTER ILLUSTRATION OF THE HIV VIRUS ATTACKING A CELL

FACT:

SCIENTISTS KNOW OF ABOUT 3,000 VIRUSES, BUT THERE ARE PROBABLY MILLIONS THAT HAVEN'T BEEN DISCOVERED.

BATTLING BACTERIA

Less than one percent of all bacteria cause disease. But when they do, they are dangerous and deadly.

THE BLACK DEATH

During the Middle Ages people experienced one of the worst disease outbreaks the world has ever seen. Between 1347 and 1352, the plague, often known as the Black Death, killed more than 25 million people. Everyone was sick or worried about getting sick.

Rats were a common sight in towns at this time. Rats carried fleas. And those fleas carried the plague bacteria. Fleas jumped from the rats onto people.

With one bite the flea's spit seeped under a person's skin. The area near the bite began to swell. This swelling, called a bubo, was reddish or black and hurt to touch. Buboes soon spread throughout the body, swelling to the size of apples. The bacteria also caused chills, high fevers, and difficulty breathing. Nearly everyone who got the disease died within a few days.

The disease spread rapidly from person to person. When a person with the bacteria coughed, the germs sprayed to anyone nearby. A couple of days later, new victims felt the symptoms.

RING AROUND THE ROSIE

Many people claim the nursery rhyme "Ring around the Rosie" describes the plague. That claim is probably false. The first printing of the rhyme was in 1881, long after the plague. But here's what the myth claims the song means:

"Ring around the rosie" describes the ring that developed around the rosy red buboes.

"A pocket full of posies" describes the flowers people carried in order to cover up the smell of rotting bodies.

"Ashes, Ashes" describes how dead bodies were burned when towns ran out of space to bury them.

"We all fall down" describes the very fast death of plague victims.

TUBERCULOSIS

Tuberculosis (TB) consumes a person from the inside. TB bacteria attack the lungs first. The disease starts with a hacking cough, fever, and pain in the chest. It's a struggle to take a breath.

Over time the bacteria attack other internal organs. Eventually a TB patient starts coughing up blood and stops eating.

Like many other diseases, TB bacteria spread when a sneeze or cough sprays spit onto other people. In the 1800s TB was the most common cause of death in the United States and Europe. Since 1800 scientists estimate that more than 1 billion people have died from TB.

CHILDREN WITH TB WERE SENT TO LIVE TOGETHER IN TUBERCULOSIS SCHOOLS.

FACT: IN THE 1800S TB WAS COMMONLY CALLED "CONSUMPTION."

CHOLERA

Death by diarrhea. Millions of people have died this way. Cholera bacteria cause a person's body to release large amounts of water in the form of severe diarrhea. Not having enough water leads to **dehydration**, vomiting, and terrible stomach cramps. If not treated, cholera can lead to a painful death.

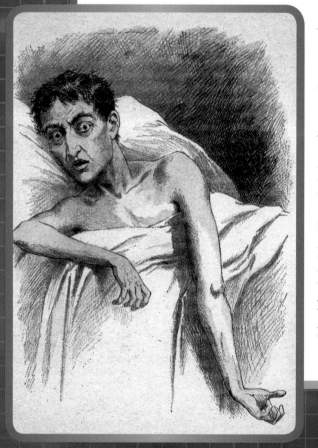

Cholera is still around, but there are fewer deaths today because people understand how the disease spreads. Cholera bacteria spread through poop. In poorer areas of the world, human waste sometimes seeps into food and water supplies. If bacteria-filled poop gets into the food or water, many people get sick.

dehydration—a life-threatening medical condition caused by a lack of water

LEPROSY

Leprosy is one of the oldest known diseases in the world. Leprosy bacteria cause lumps all over a person's body. They also cause nerve damage and weakness in the arms and legs.

For thousands of years, people were terrified of the disease. They assumed it was highly contagious. People with leprosy were sent to live in leper colonies, far away from friends and family.

Scientists now know that leprosy is not very contagious. It is spread by coughing or sneezing. But a person has to come in contact with the bacteria many times before he or she becomes infected.

PATIENT INFECTED WITH LEPROSY

contagious—easy to catch or spread   infected—filled with bacteria or viruses

NECROTIZING FASCIITIS

Leprosy definitely isn't a disease you want to get. But it might be better than necrotizing fasciitis (NF).

NF is an infection caused by a nasty bacteria. This bacteria attacks skin and tissue, appearing to eat the flesh. NF is rare. But when it happens, it causes extreme pain, high fever, and dehydration. Eventually, the skin turns black and dies. About 25 percent of people who get NF die. If victims survive, doctors might have to remove their arms or legs.

TYPHUS

Fleas really are pests when it comes to disease. They helped spread the plague. A flea bite can also spread typhus bacteria. Lice and ticks can also carry the disease.

Sometimes called jail fever, typhus is an ancient disease. It occurs most often in places where people live close together. This close living, as well as a lack of washing, often attracts fleas.

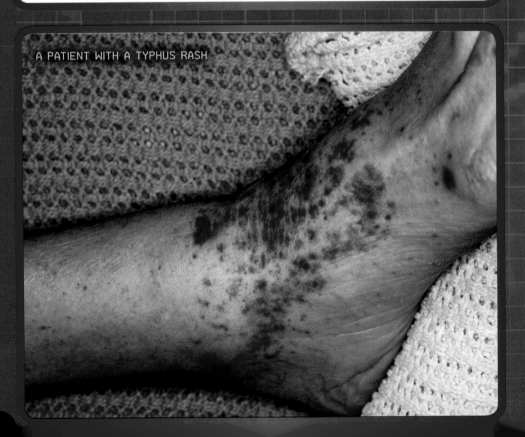
A PATIENT WITH A TYPHUS RASH

About 10 days after a person is bitten, symptoms start. The disease begins with a headache, fever, chills, and upset stomach. About four days later, the tell-tale red typhus rash appears. By the end of the week, the fever can be as high as 106 degrees Fahrenheit (41 degrees Celsius). The fever rages for almost two full weeks before quickly falling back to normal.

If not treated typhus can cause the blood to flow slower than normal. Flesh on the fingers, ears, and nose dies. Other patients have kidney failure or go into comas. But if treated, very few people die of typhus.

TYPHOID FEVER

Typhus and typhoid fever are often confused. But they are different diseases. Typhoid bacteria pass from person to person through food and water. If someone with the disease handles food you eat, you could be infected.

During the U.S. Civil War (1861–1865), typhoid fever was common. Soldiers with typhoid fever had diarrhea, high fevers, and a rash of rose-colored spots. At least 60,000 soldiers died of typhoid fever.

VICIOUS VIRUSES

Viruses are more common than bacterial diseases. They can be more troublesome too. Viruses can't be cured by antibiotics, so these diseases are often harder to stop.

INFLUENZA

One virus everyone knows about is the flu. What makes the flu so dangerous is how easily it spreads.

There have been several flu **pandemics** throughout history. One of the worst arrived in Boston, Massachusetts, in 1918. From Boston the virus spread across the country. During the outbreak millions of people were sick. Schools and public buildings closed. Cities shut down services such as garbage collection. The virus that year was the strongest the world had ever seen. Many people could not fight it off. By the end of the year, between 20 and 50 million people worldwide had died of the flu.

pandemic—a disease that spreads over a wide area and affects many people

THE INFLUENZA VIRUS CHANGES EACH YEAR. IN 2009 A NEW INFLUENZA VIRUS APPEARED. CALLED H1N1, IT INFECTED ALMOST ONE IN EVERY FIVE PEOPLE IN THE UNITED STATES.

SCHOOL GYMS WERE USED AS HOSPITALS DURING THE 1918 FLU PANDEMIC.

SMALLPOX

Smallpox was a dangerous, easy-to-catch virus. Since the earliest known case in ancient Egypt, smallpox has killed close to 500 million people.

The smallpox virus caused crusty pink scabs on the skin. These painful, itchy sores covered a person's entire body. As an added bonus, smallpox also gave sufferers backaches, diarrhea, high fevers, and vomiting.

Smallpox spread through people's spit. Anyone standing in a room where an infected person coughed, sneezed, or even talked could get infected. The disease was particularly dangerous for children. Eighty percent of children under age 5 who caught smallpox died.

But there's good news! Scientists invented a **vaccine** for smallpox. Because of worldwide vaccination, the disease no longer exists. It is the only human disease to be completely erased.

vaccine—a medicine that prevents a disease

FACT:

SCIENTISTS BELIEVE THAT SMALLPOX KILLED 95 PERCENT OF THE AMERICAN INDIAN POPULATION. WHEN EUROPEANS FIRST CAME TO AMERICA, THEY CARRIED THE VIRUS WITH THEM AND PASSED IT TO THE INDIANS.

POLIO

Ask someone who lived during the 1940s and 1950s what disease people feared most. The answer would be polio. Anyone could catch the polio virus, but it attacked children the most.

The polio virus attacks the nervous system. At first an infected person might have a fever, headache, vomiting, and stiffness in the neck. But just a few hours after infection, the virus attacks the spinal cord. It paralyzes a person's legs. In some cases the virus also paralyzes the breathing muscles. If that happens a person can no longer breathe on his or her own.

In some people the virus leaves lasting effects. Some remain paralyzed for the rest of their lives. Most suffer with a permanent limp. Kids in the United States don't worry about polio much today, though. Because of a very successful vaccine, almost no one has had polio in the United States since 1979. But polio is still a problem in some poorer countries.

FACT:

PRESIDENT FRANKLIN D. ROOSEVELT CAUGHT POLIO WHEN HE WAS 39. HE HAD TO USE LEG BRACES AND A WHEELCHAIR THE REST OF HIS LIFE.

So how does such a horrible virus spread? The polio virus lives in a person's poop. Imagine that a boy carrying the virus doesn't wash his hands after using the rest room. Then he touches the doorknob as he leaves. He has just left the virus there for the next person who opens the door. After touching the doorknob, another person puts his finger in his mouth to bite off a hangnail. The virus enters his body and infects him. Now do you see why washing hands is so important?

PATIENTS WITH POLIO WERE PUT IN SEPARATE SECTIONS OF HOSPITALS TO KEEP THE DISEASE FROM SPREADING.

YELLOW FEVER

Fleas and lice aren't the only pests to spread disease. Mosquitoes can be deadly pests too. One virus mosquitoes spread is yellow fever.

Yellow fever develops a few days after a bite from an infected mosquito. At first the victim gets a headache and muscle aches. Fever, vomiting, and loss of appetite are quick to follow. After three or four days, the symptoms disappear. Once symptoms disappear most people are over the virus.

But an unlucky few will develop into a second stage of yellow fever. At this point people suffer heart, liver, and kidney failure. These failures give the person's skin a yellow color.

Today the disease is most often found in Africa and Latin America. If you're traveling there, ask your doctor for the yellow fever vaccine.

MALARIA

Need another reason to be wary of mosquitoes? These flying germ-carriers can also carry a parasite that causes malaria.

A person with malaria will have a high fever, nausea, headache, and blood in their poop. More than 1 million people die each year from this dangerous disease.

parasite—an animal that lives inside another animal and causes harm

RABIES

This next virus is not spread by mosquitoes. But it is spread by a bite. The rabies virus lives in the spit of an infected mammal. At one time dogs were the most common mammals to spread the disease. Today most pets get vaccinated. Bites from wild animals such as foxes or skunks are now the most common cause of rabies.

Once bitten by an infected animal, the rabies virus affects a person quickly. The virus travels from the open wound through the person's bloodstream. It doesn't take long to travel to the brain. Before long, rabies causes drooling, shaking, and difficulty swallowing.

If the infected person gets the vaccine soon after the bite, he or she will be fine. But without the shot, the respiratory system shuts down. The person will die about a week after symptoms begin.

WILD ANIMALS SUCH AS SKUNKS GET THE RABIES VIRUS IF BITTEN BY ANOTHER INFECTED ANIMAL.

MENINGITIS

Meningitis is a scary disease that causes fluid around the brain and spinal cord to swell. It can cause severe brain damage and death, even if a person gets treatment right away.

Meningitis can actually be caused by either a virus or bacteria. The bacterial form of meningitis is especially dangerous. Bacteria pass from person to person by coughing, sneezing, or kissing. Living in close quarters, such as college dorms, can help the bacteria spread too. For this reason some colleges require students to get the meningitis vaccine.

THE GREEN ARROWS SHOW HOW BACTERIAL MENINGITIS SPREADS THROUGH THE BRAIN.

MYSTERIOUS CAUSES

Viruses or bacteria don't cause all diseases. Some are caused by the way your genes are formed. Others have causes that doctors are still trying to understand.

CREUTZFELDT–JAKOB DISEASE

Creutzfeldt–Jakob disease (CJD) causes a normal cell to attack the brain. As the disease eats away at the brain, the victim loses his or her memory.

As the disease gets worse, the person's behavior and personality change. Within six months the victim loses his or her eyesight and starts seeing things that aren't really there. Eventually, the person falls into a coma, stops breathing, and dies.

There is no cure for CJD. It mostly affects people over age 60, and it kills almost everyone infected within a year. No one knows exactly what causes CJD.

SCIENTISTS STUDY PIECES OF THE BRAIN AFFECTED BY CJD TO TRY TO UNDERSTAND THE DISEASE.

AMYOTROPHIC LATERAL SCLEROSIS

Amyotrophic Lateral Sclerosis (ALS) is a genetic disease that affects the brain. ALS makes nerve cells in the brain and spinal cord wither and die. When the cells die, they no longer send messages to the body. Body parts and functions shut down. The disease causes total paralysis. Eventually the patient can't breathe and dies.

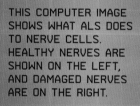

THIS COMPUTER IMAGE SHOWS WHAT ALS DOES TO NERVE CELLS. HEALTHY NERVES ARE SHOWN ON THE LEFT, AND DAMAGED NERVES ARE ON THE RIGHT.

FACT:

LOU GEHRIG WAS A BASEBALL PLAYER FOR THE NEW YORK YANKEES FROM 1925 TO 1939. GEHRIG WAS DIAGNOSED WITH ALS IN 1939. TODAY MANY PEOPLE CALL ALS "LOU GEHRIG'S DISEASE."

A tiny shift in a person's genetic code before birth can cause the body to develop some rare conditions.

PROGERIA (PREMATURE AGING SYNDROME)

Progeria is a genetic condition caused by a gene **mutation**. Progeria causes rapid aging in children. Imagine having wrinkled skin and a weak heart—all before you're 10 years old. It's very rare. There are only about 50 cases in the United States. Children with progeria don't grow normally. They typically die of heart disease before their 13th birthday.

A 12-YEAR-OLD GIRL WITH PROGERIA

mutation—a change from the original gene

HYPERTRICHOSIS (WEREWOLF SYNDROME)

Hypertrichosis is another disease that changes the body's appearance. A person with hypertrichosis grows hair all over his or her body. There are fewer than 100 cases worldwide, and it often runs in families. In the past people with hypertrichosis often worked in carnivals.

SCARY SCIENCE

Bacteria and viruses lurk in every corner of the world. Insects and animals carry hidden germs. Even the tiniest tweak in our genetic code can cause disease. That's truly scary science!

But understanding diseases and how they spread can make them less scary. Some diseases can be avoided by simple hand washing or avoiding people who are sick. Today we have vaccines that protect us from some of the most dangerous illnesses too.

Doctors have solved many medical mysteries. And they are hard at work solving the scary science mysteries that remain.

GLOSSARY

contagious (kun-TAY-juss)—easy to catch or spread

dehydration (dee-hy-DRAY-shuhn)—a life-threatening medical condition caused by a lack of water

gene (JEEN)—a part of every cell that carries physical and behavioral information passed from parents to their children

infected (in-FEKT-uhd)—filled with bacteria or viruses

microbe (MYE-krobe)—a tiny living thing that is too small to be seen without a microscope

mutation (myoo-TAY-shuhn)—a change from the original gene

pandemic (pan-DEM-ik)—a disease that spreads over a wide area and affects many people

parasite (PAIR-uh-site)—an animal or plant that lives on or inside another animal or plant and causes harm

vaccine (vak-SEEN)—a medicine that prevents a disease

READ MORE

Donovan, Sandra. *Rumble & Spew: Gross Stuff in Your Stomach and Intestines*. Gross Body Science. Minneapolis: Millbrook Press, 2010.

Keyser, Amber J. *Anatomy of a Pandemic*. Disasters. Mankato, Minn.: Capstone Press, 2011.

Reingold, Adam. *Smallpox: Is It Over?* Nightmare Plagues. New York: Bearport Pub., 2011.

INTERNET SITES

FactHound offers a safe, fun way to find Internet sites related to this book. All of the sites on FactHound have been researched by our staff.

Here's all you do:

Visit *www.facthound.com*

Type in this code: 9781476539270

Super-cool stuff!

Check out projects, games and lots more at
www.capstonekids.com

INDEX